14.20

Y0-DWO-390

DATE DUE

JUN 1 - 1999	
FEB 8 - 2000	
FEB 8 - 2000	
5/12/2000	OCT 1 0 2005
DEC 2 7 2000	
	APR 1 7 2006
FEB 1 4 2001	
JUN 1 1 2001	MAY 3 1 2006
FEB 1 6 2002	
MAY 1 3 2003	
JAN 3 0 2003	
JUN 2 8 2005	

DEMCO INC 38-2931

JAN 0 4 1999

The United States

Pennsylvania

Anne Welsbacher
ABDO & Daughters

visit us at
www.abdopub.com

Published by Abdo & Daughters, 4940 Viking Drive, Suite 622, Edina, Minnesota 55435.
Copyright © 1998 by Abdo Consulting Group, Inc., Pentagon Tower, P.O. Box 36036,
Minneapolis, Minnesota 55435 USA. International copyrights reserved in all countries. No
part of this book may be reproduced in any form without written permission from the pub-
lisher.

Printed in the United States.

Cover and Interior Photo credits: Peter Arnold, Inc., SuperStock, Archive

Edited by Lori Kinstad Pupeza
Contributing editor Brooke Henderson
Special thanks to our Checkerboard Kids—Aisha Baker, Annie O'Leary, Morgan Roberts,
Shane Wagner

All statistics taken from the 1990 census; The Rand McNally Discovery Atlas of The United
States.

Library of Congress Cataloging-in-Publication Data

Welsbacher, Anne, 1955-
    Pennsylvania / Anne Welsbacher.
    p. cm. -- (United States)
    Includes index.
    Summary: A brief introduction to the geography, history, natural resources,
    industries, cities, and people of Pennsylvania.
    ISBN 1-56239-893-8
    1. Pennsylvania--Juvenile literature. [1. Pennsylvania.] I. Title. II. Series:
    United States (Series)
    F149.3.W44 1998
    974.8--dc21   97-36202
                                                                                           CIP
                                                                                          AC

Contents

Welcome to Pennsylvania

The world's largest chocolate **factory** is in Pennsylvania! The state is famous for making many other things, too.

Pennsylvania is next to one of the Great Lakes. It has pretty rivers, hills, lakes, and rich land for farming.

The United States first said it was a new country in Pennsylvania. People rang the Liberty Bell to share the news. The bell is still on display today.

Pennsylvania was one of the early **colonies** in the United States. On a map, the colonies look like stones in a bridge. Pennsylvania was right in the middle—the most important, or "key" place in the bridge. So Pennsylvania is called the Keystone State.

Kids touching the Liberty Bell in Philadelphia, Pennsylvania.

Fast Facts

Pennsylvania is one of the original 13 colonies.

13

PENNSYLVANIA

Capital
Harrisburg (52,376 people)
Area
44,892 square miles
(116,270 sq km)
Population
11,924,710 people
Rank: 5th
Statehood
December 12, 1787
(2nd state admitted)
Principal rivers
Allegheny River, Delaware River,
Ohio River, Susquehanna River
Highest point
Mount Davis;
3,213 feet (979 m)
Largest city
Philadelphia (1,585,577 people)
Motto
Virtue, liberty, and independence
Famous People
Andrew Carnegie, Bill Cosby,
Stephen Foster, Martha Graham,
Benjamin West

*S*tate Flag

*M*ountain
Laurel

*H*emlock

*R*uffed Grouse

About Pennsylvania

The Keystone State

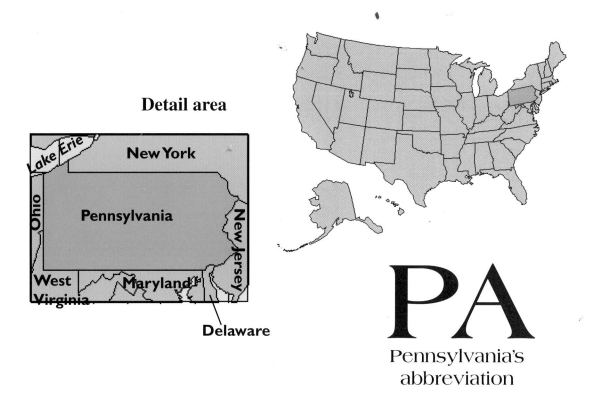

Detail area

Lake Erie · New York · Ohio · Pennsylvania · New Jersey · West Virginia · Maryland · Delaware

PA

Pennsylvania's abbreviation

Borders: west (Ohio), north (Lake Erie, New York), east (New Jersey), south (Maryland, West Virginia, Delaware)

Pennsylvania's Treasures

Pennsylvania's land is good for farming. Some of its land is the best in the eastern part of the country! The soil is rich and there is much water.

In some parts the soil is rocky. Some soil is mixed with gravel and sand. Soil in other parts of the state has limestone and shale.

There are many minerals in the ground, too. Hard coal and soft coal are in much of Pennsylvania's land. Iron and gas also are mined from the land.

Opposite page:
A farm in
Pennsylvania.

Beginnings

Early people in Pennsylvania were the **Lenni-Lenape** and the **Susquehannocks**. In the 1600s, **Dutch** and Swedish settlers came. Later, people from England came.

Pennsylvania was one of 13 English **colonies**. The English and the French fought over the colonies. The colonies wanted to be a new, free country.

Leaders met in Philadelphia, Pennsylvania, and signed the Declaration of Independence. Then they rang a big bell called the Liberty Bell. It was a **symbol** for freedom.

They fought the Revolutionary War with England. The colonies won. They became the United States of America.

Much fighting went on in Pennsylvania. Farmers grew food for the soldiers and horses. **Factories** made powder for guns.

In 1787, Pennsylvania became the second state. In the 1800s, railroads were built across Pennsylvania mountains.

From 1861 to 1865, the Civil War was fought. This time it was about slavery. Southern states wanted slavery. Pennsylvania and other northern states did not.

Once more, much fighting was in Pennsylvania, and Pennsylvania again helped out. **Factories** made guns, bullets, and clothing for uniforms. Many Pennsylvanians helped African Americans escape from slavery.

In the late 1800s, Pennsylvania had more coal mining than in any other state. More immigrants came to Pennsylvania from Europe.

In 1979, there was a threat of a **radiation** leak at a factory called Three Mile Island. Since then, Pennsylvanians have worked hard to make their state clean and safe. In 1985, Pittsburgh, Pennsylvania, was called the best place to live in the whole country!

A Civil War battle scene in Pennsylvania.

B.C. to 1750s

Early Pennsylvania

 10,000 B.C.-1600s: The people living in Pennsylvania include the **Lenni-Lenape**, the Monongahela, and the **Susquehannocks**.

 1600s: The **Quakers** settle in Pennsylvania. They trade and live peacefully with Native American people.

 1754: The first of the French and Indian Wars is fought.

Pennsylvania

B.C. to 1750s

1770s to 1780s

Hard-won Freedom

1774: Colonists meet in Philadelphia to talk about making a new country. Soon they are at war with England.

1776: Philadelphia becomes the first capital of the United States. The Declaration of Independence is signed in Philadelphia.

1777: The U.S. Army, headed by General George Washington, is beaten by the English in the Battle of Brandywine in Pennsylvania. Disease and cold weather make the winter very hard.

1781: The **colonies** win the Revolutionary War. They are helped by Pennsylvania soldiers, farmers, and **manufacturers**.

14

Pennsylvania

1770s to 1780s

1787 to Today

New Country, New Freedoms

 1787: Pennsylvania becomes the second state of the United States.

 1800s: Railroads and canals in Pennsylvania help connect eastern United States to the West.

 1863: More than 50,000 people are hurt or killed in the Battle of Gettysburg in Pennsylvania during the Civil War.

 1941: Pennsylvanians build ships and make uniforms and chocolate bars for American soldiers fighting in World War II.

Pennsylvania

1787 to Today

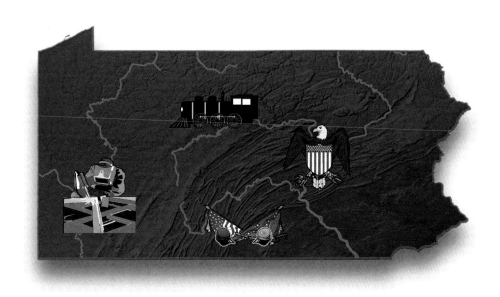

Pennsylvania's People

There are almost 12 million people living in Pennsylvania. Almost four million people live in **rural** areas. This is more than in any other state.

Mr. Rogers is from Latrobe, Pennsylvania. He likes to sing "Won't you be my neighbor?" on his TV show. Bill Cosby is from Philadelphia. He is in movies and TV shows. He tells jokes and stories about children.

The singers in the group Boyz II Men are from Philadelphia. So are singers Chubby Checker and Patti LaBelle.

W.C. Fields, who made many funny movies, was from Philadelphia. And the famous actors Michael Keaton and John and Ethel Barrymore were from Pennsylvania. Drew Barrymore is an actor from the new **generation** of the long Barrymore family.

Baseball star Reggie Jackson is from Pennsylvania.
Other Pennsylvania sports stars are legendary football
player Jim Thorpe, future Hall of Fame quarterbacks Joe
Montana and Dan Marino, and one of the greatest
golfers ever, Arnold Palmer.

Boyz II Men

Bill Cosby

Mr. Rogers

Pennsylvania's Cities

Philadelphia is the largest city in Pennsylvania. It also is one of the largest cities in the United States! Many coins are made in Philadelphia at a **mint**.

Pittsburgh is the next biggest city. Lake Erie is next to Erie, Pennsylvania.

Harrisburg is the capital of Pennsylvania. The town of Altoona has a railroad museum with lots of trains.

In Punxsutawney, Pennsylvania, people watch a groundhog every February to see how much longer winter will last. And the world's largest chocolate **factory** is in Hershey, Pennsylvania!

Erie

Scranton

Allentown

Pittsburgh

Harrisburg

Philadelphia

20

Downtown Pittsburgh, Pennsylvania.

Pennsylvania's Land

Pennsylvania is near water in every direction! Lake Erie is on one side and the Atlantic Ocean is close to the other side. Pennsylvania has seven different regions.

The Lake Plains region is a very small area in the northwest corner of the state. It borders Lake Erie. It has beaches and very fertile land.

The biggest region in the state is the Allegheny Plateau. It covers all of northern and western Pennsylvania except for the Lake Plains region. It has mountains, rivers, and many streams.

The Valley and Ridge region is the second biggest region. This region also has many rivers and mountains. It is cut by many long valleys.

Lake Plains

Allegheny Plateau

Valley and Ridge

New England Upland

Piedmont Plateau

Coastal Plain

Blue Ridge

The New England Upland and the Blue Ridge regions are two tiny areas in the state. Their regions are mostly found in neighboring states.

The Piedmont Plateau is a large area in the southeastern part of the state. Low hills and pretty valleys fill this region. This area also has good farmland.

The Coastal Plain covers a small region in the far southeastern part of the state. It is a low fertile area near the Atlantic Ocean.

Pennsylvania has many forests. In them are hemlock, beech, hickory, maple, pine, black cherry, and tulip trees.

Susquehanna River, in Hyner, Pennsylvania.

Pennsylvania at Play

Pennsylvanians enjoy many sports. The Pittsburgh Pirates and the Philadelphia Phillies play big-league baseball in Pennsylvania. The Pittsburgh Steelers and the Philadelphia Eagles are the state's football teams.

The Philadelphia 76ers shoot baskets for Pennsylvania fans. The Little League World Series baseball game is played every August in Williamsport, Pennsylvania.

Every New Year's Day Pennsylvanians enjoy the Mummers' Parade in Philadelphia. The parade is a mix of customs from Germany and from Africa. Many Pennsylvanians once came from these countries. The parade includes dances, costumes, and music.

Orchestras in Pittsburgh and Philadelphia are world famous. An orchestra is a music group with violins, horns, harps, drums, and many other instruments.

There are many museums and areas about history in Pennsylvania. At Gettysburg, visitors can see where the battle of Gettysburg took place and where President Lincoln gave his most famous speech.

Pennsylvania has many parks and forests. The Allegheny National Forest is a big forest in northern Pennsylvania. In the Kittatinny Mountains is a hawk **sanctuary** where birds of prey can be seen.

Gettysburg National Battlefield, Pennsylvania.

Pennsylvania at Work

Most Pennsylvanians work in service. They work in banks, stores, or places that tourists visit.

Pennsylvania is one of the leading states in the country in **manufacturing**. Pennsylvanians make ice cream, chocolate, and paint.

Many people mine the coal from the ground. They also mine limestone, gas, and oil.

Some Pennsylvanians work for the railroad or the turnpike. Others are farmers. They raise chickens, pigs, and dairy cows for milk.

Opposite page: A farm in Lancaster County, Pennsylvania.

Fun Facts

•Each February 2, everyone in the United States watches a groundhog named Punxsutawney Phil to see if he will see his shadow when he comes out of his hole in Punxsutawney, Pennsylvania. If he sees his own shadow and runs back into his hole, there will be six more weeks of winter. If he doesn't have a shadow, spring will come soon. This event is called Groundhog Day.

•The Slinky toy was invented in Pennsylvania. So were banana splits and Hershey bars.

•Pennsylvanian Robert Fulton invented the first working steamboat. It took to water in 1807.

•The ice cream soda was invented in Philadelphia in 1874. A man who made drinks from cream, syrup, and fizzy water ran out of cream. So he tried ice cream. It was a big hit!

- People in south Pennsylvania who are called Pennsylvania Dutch are not really **Dutch**. They are German. The German word for "German" is *Deutsch* (pronounced DOY-ch). When they first settled in Pennsylvania, other people thought they were saying they were Dutch.
- The world's biggest chocolate **factory** is in Hershey, Pennsylvania. The Hershey Plant began in 1905.
- "Pittsburgh" once was spelled without the letter "H" at the end.
- The first magazine in the **colonies** in America was in Philadelphia. It was called *The American Magazine, or a Monthly View of the British Colonies*. It was printed in 1741.

A Pennsylvania groundhog.

Glossary

Chemicals: the parts in things; chemistry is putting the parts together to make other things.

Claim: to take.

College: a school you can go to after high school.

Colony: a place that is owned by another country, even if it is far away.

Dutch: people of the Netherlands.

Factory: a big building where things are made.

Generation: one age group in a family; a grandmother is a generation, her daughter is another, and her daughter is a third generation.

Lenni-Lenape: people who once lived in Pennsylvania; the name means "original people."

Manufacture: to make things.

Mint: a factory where money is made.

Orchestra: a music group with violins, horns, harps, drums, and many other instruments.

Plateau: a high, flat area of land.

Quaker: a church that began in the 1600s; Quakers believe in freedom of religion and in peaceful actions.

Radiation: powerful and dangerous rays that are sent out.

Rural: on farms or in other areas away from cities.

Sanctuary: a place where wildlife is kept safe.

Secede: to break away.

Susquehannock: Native Americans who once lived in Pennsylvania; the name means "people of well-watered land."

Symbol: something that makes you think of something else; the Liberty Bell is a symbol for freedom.

Internet Sites

Spirit of 76
http://spiritof76.com/index.html#bookmark
This site takes you to the Crossroads of the Revolution. This site has things to do, places to go, at your service, trail of history, and much more. Good information for anyone interested in Pennsylvania.

The One-room Schoolhouse
http://www.msc.cornell.edu/~weeds/SchoolPages/welcome.html
The One-room School Homepage is dedicated to remembering the way of life practiced by the students, teachers and community of the Caldwell School. Even though its doors are now closed and no classes are being taught, we all can learn something from this school and its people. This site is interesting with many, many links.

These sites are subject to change. Go to your favorite search engine and type in Pennsylvania for more sites.

PASS IT ON

Tell Others Something Special About Your State

To educate readers around the country, pass on interesting tips, places to see, history, and little unknown facts about the state you live in. We want to hear from you!

To get posted on ABDO & Daughters website, e-mail us at "mystate@abdopub.com"

Index

A

animals 23
Atlantic Ocean 22

C

chocolate 4, 16, 20, 26, 29
Civil War 11, 16
coal 8, 11, 26
colonies 4, 10, 14, 29

D

Declaration of Independence 10
Dutch 10, 29

E

England 10, 14
Europe 11, 19

F

factory 4, 20, 29
farming 4, 8
forests 22, 25
French 10, 12

G

gas 8, 26
Gettysburg 16, 25
Great Lakes 4

H

Harrisburg 6, 20
Hershey 20, 28, 29
history 25

I

immigrants 11

K

keystone 4, 7

L

Lake Erie 7, 20, 22
lakes 4
land 4, 8
Lenni-Lenape 10
Liberty Bell 4, 10

M

manufacturing 26
mountains 10, 22, 25

P

Philadelphia 76ers 24
Philadelphia Eagles 24
Philadelphia Phillies 24
Pittsburgh 11, 19, 20, 24, 29
Pittsburgh Pirates 24

Pittsburgh Steelers 24
President Lincoln 25

Q

Quakers 12

R

railroads 10, 16
Revolutionary War 10
rivers 4, 6

S

settlers 10
slavery 11
soil 8
Swedish 10

T

Three Mile Island 11

W

Washington, George 14
water 8, 22, 28